Oracle for anxiety

Grete Stars

No part of this work may be reproduced, incorporated into a computer system, or transmitted in any form or by any means (electronic, mechanical, photocopying, recording or otherwise) without the prior written permission of the copyright holders. Infringement of such rights may constitute an intellectual property crime.
Oracle for anxiety © Grete Stars, 2023

This Oracle has been created to guide you and help you walk the path of life when you are suffering from anxiety.

Often, uncertainty stalks us and generates more stress.

This is an Oracle created to give you answers while keeping you calm and making you see that there is no hurry, that everything is fine, that you are well, anchored to the calm and serene wisdom of life.

Thanks to the Oracle you will have answers that will gently invite you to action or inaction, but always with your well-being and your calm above all.

A new path of peace begins.

How to use this Oracle?

Two simple ways of extracting wisdom from the Oracle are provided.

Both begin with a moment of reflection and calm in which you ask yourself a question. Take a deep breath and proceed to take one of these two actions:

- Pick up the book and randomly open any of its pages. The answer will be right in front of you.

- Open the book to the next page and with your eyes closed let your finger select a number, then turn to the page with that same number. The answer will be revealed.

It is no longer up to you. Set your mind on a new goal.

1

Take the smallest possible step.

2

At this very moment, leaving it alone is the wisest thing to do.

3

Someone close to you has the answer.

Open channels of communication.

4

Do not force drastic changes.

Plan quietly and with confidence in the future.

5

Take distance.

Good time for a reconciliation (with yourself or with another).

6

A tiny step can open big doors.

Boldness and confidence are your allies.

You will know how to assert your arguments and they will be accepted without objection.

8

Conditions are not favorable. Wait patiently for your moment.

9

Your beliefs radiate great calmness. Your entourage supports you.

Go for it.

Do not worry about things that have not happened. The path is clear and it is propitious to move forward.

11

Look after your well-being and dedicate time to your mind and body. The rest must wait.

If you are true to yourself, the world will be full of gifts for you. Don't give in to someone else's pressures.

13

Time will prove you right.

Wait 7 days and plant your seed.

Moving forward brings misfortune. The road ends in a precipice. New challenges will blossom.

Build new social relationships that will open your mind.

Good fortune will come from there.

Balance your emotional side with your rational side.

Therein lies the light that will guide you on this path.

Not everything that seems to be, is.

Caution.

18

Advance without fear but without destroying alliances.

19

Use your imagination and you will succeed. You are more powerful than you think.

20

Time is not propitious.

Stopping now is wise.

21

Nature desires your happiness.

Interiorize this reflection and happiness will be with you.

Accept what is not in your hand to change.

Take the only small but firm step you can take now.

23

Save important decisions for a more serene time.

Give you a moment to take care of yourself.

24

Observe the past in order to process it.

Moving forward in this way is conducive.

25

Others may not understand how you feel.

Trust yourself and do what you know is right.

26

The answer is NO.

27

What you think is a noble ideal may be an impulsive decision. Meditate the idea for 7 days.

28

The Energy is fully available to act or speak loud and clear.

29

Lower your expectations and appreciate what you have.

You don't need what you think you need.

30

Go deep into what you feel. Out of the darkness you can reveal much light.

It is time for transformation.

31

Communicate from vulnerability and you will receive crucial support to achieve what you long for.

It is time to make decisions but only for the long term.

Recognize your progress.

33

Don't initiate exhausting tasks. Sometimes small steps lead to higher peaks.

34

There is an external pressure that polishes your diamond.

The resulting light is powerful and favorable.

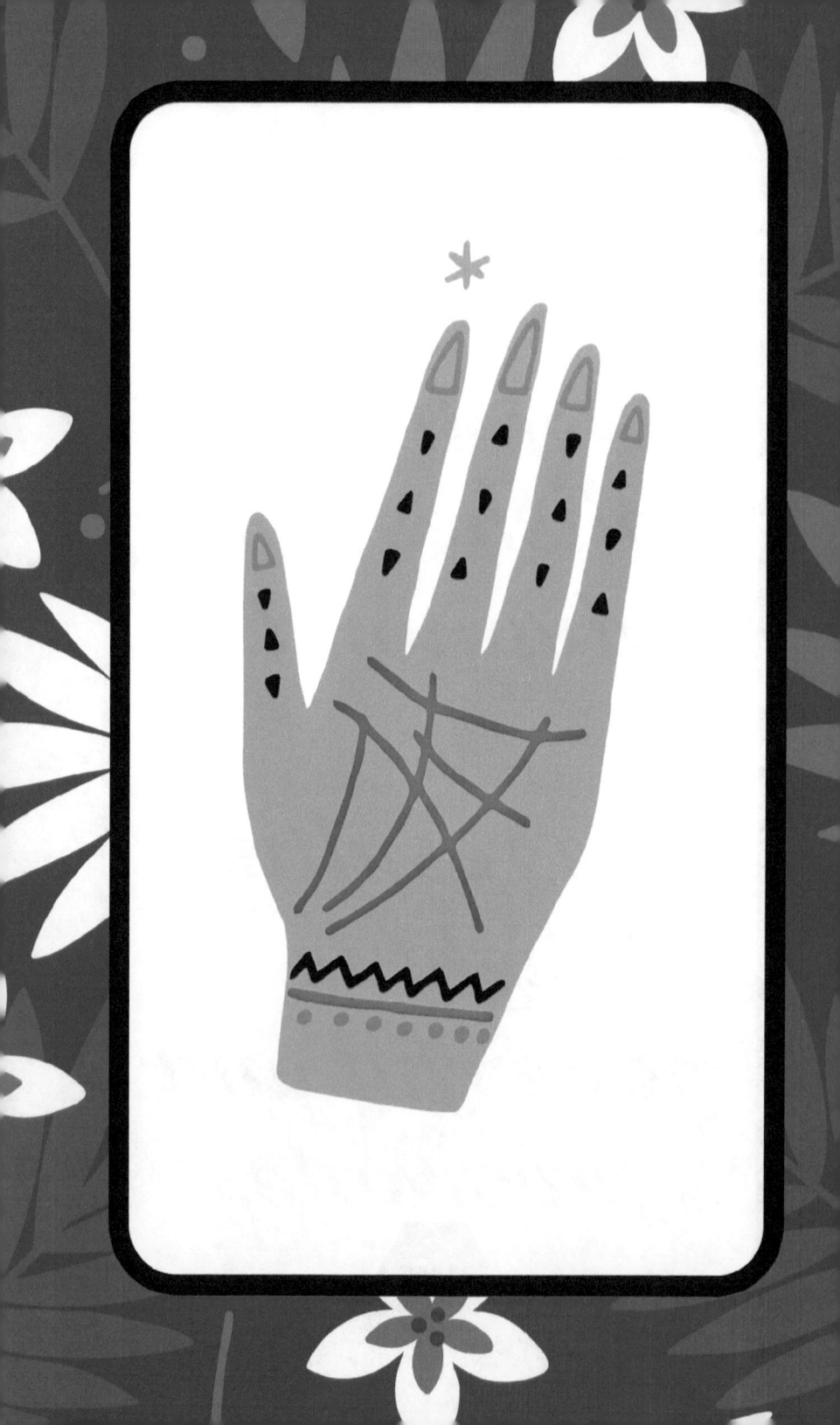

What you see is what you get.

Use your confidence to advance intimate goals.

36

Innovate, create new methods. Originality leads you hand in hand to success.

Believe in yourself.

What you resist, persists.

Accept what you feel and proactively lead yourself to transform internally.

There is tension between what you think and what you feel.

Communicate tactfully with yourself and others and take action in 3 days.

Don't get lost in unfounded fantasies.

Before you act, meditate on whether your desire is based on old fears or hidden feelings.

NOTES

NOTES

NOTES

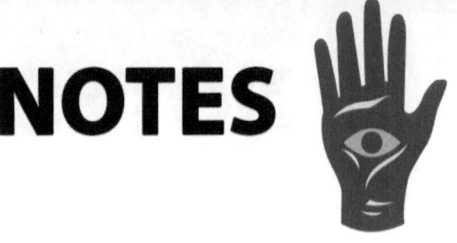

NOTES

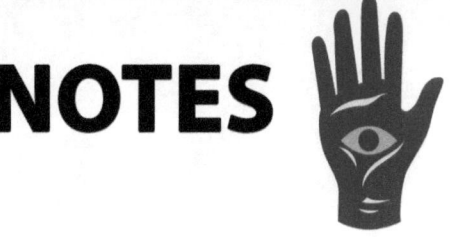

www.ingramcontent.com/pod-product-compliance
Lightning Source LLC
LaVergne TN
LVHW041625070526
838199LV00052B/3245